D1714184

THE CBT RESILIENCE JOURNAL:

21 DAYS TOWARD DEVELOPING IMMUNITY TO ADVERSITY IN A PANDEMIC ERA

Jeff Riggenbach, PhD
jeffriggenbach.com
clincialtoolboxset.com

INTRODUCTION

They say what doesn't kill us makes us stronger. This isn't always the case. People react differently to adversity. We now know that biology even plays a role in how we respond to stressors in life.

But whether you are a boxer absorbing blows, an average citizen getting rocked by this pandemic, a trauma victim, or simply somebody living one of a thousand other scenarios who has had multiple setbacks in life, there are some common characteristics in those who succumb versus those who survive, those who fall down versus those who stand up, those who turn it in versus those who turn it on, and those who throw in the towel versus those who throw another punch.

Resilience has been defined as the *ability to adjust to or easily recover from challenges or misfortune.* Some research suggests it takes 21 days to develop resilience. There are many factors influencing a person's capacity to respond to stress. While far from comprehensive, this simple journal will help you facilitate the development of one habit important for resiliency each day for the next 21 days. So while what doesn't kill us doesn't always make us stronger - it can. But only if we approach it in the right way. The next 21 days will help you do just that. I wish you well in your journey to not only survive, but to thrive in these challenging times.

THE STRUGGLE IS REAL

 ## Motivational Message

"Show me someone who knows how to struggle – who isn't caught in the hold of his luxuries." - Rich Mullins

My Musings

The reality is that some people experience more adversity in life than others. If one has never been knocked down, they don't know what it is like to have to learn to get back up. Write down and reflect on past heartaches you have endured in your life.

_____

_____

_____

_____

_____

 ## Mindset Matters

While nobody asks to go through painful experiences, the process of facing and conquering life's challenges can form the basis for developing an empathy, compassion, and "stick-to-itiveness" that

those who haven't had to struggle can never fully know.

Revisit the obstacles you listed. How did overcoming each shape your thinking today? Reflect on any changes you'd like to make to your mindset to more effectively harness lessons learned from your past struggles to build resilience for the future.

_____

_____

_____

_____

_____

✔️ *Make it Happen*

Having reflected on lessons learned from my past struggles, I will commit to the following action steps:

1. _____

2. _____

3. _____

ACKNOWLEDGE LOSSES

 Motivational Message

"There was no need to be ashamed of tears, for tears bore witness that a man had the greatest courage – the courage to suffer." - Viktor Frankl

My Musings

This one is simple, but not easy. Grieve what needs to be grieved. Acknowledge loss. Admit pain. If we aren't vulnerable enough to acknowledge that we have hurt in the past, we can't learn the lessons needed to move forward in a healthy way in the future. Reflect on your feelings about previous hurts and losses.

_____

_____

_____

_____

_____

 Mindset Matters

Some people were raised with the message that sharing these types of emotions was sign of weakness. But pretending things are OK when

they are far from OK is counterproductive for building resilience.

As you honestly deal with your losses and hurts, revisit the question "based upon what I have gone through, how can I shift my mindset to cultivate resilience?

_____

_____

_____

_____

_____

✓ Make it Happen

Having honestly acknowledged the pain from my past, I commit to move forward by taking the following action steps to build my resilience:

1. _____

2. _____

3. _____

CLARITY REGARDING MISTAKES

 ## *Motivational Message*

"Mistakes are always forgivable if one has the courage to admit them."
- Bruce Lee

 ## *My Musings*

If we don't realize what exactly we did wrong, we can't know how to examine what to do different next time. As you examine adversity from previous life experiences, consider what role your choices played in contributing to the difficulties you went through.

_____

_____

_____

_____

_____

 ## *Mindset Matters*

This sounds simple enough, but very few of us are able to assign blame where it rightfully belongs. Many are prone to blame others more than is fair and most actually blame themselves more than is fair. In an attempt to develop this clarity, reflect on your previous struggles and whether or not you were taking too much responsibility for what happened versus not enough. Ask trusted others for their input.

_____

_____

_____

_____

_____

✓ *Make it Happen*

Based upon my newfound clarity regarding my actual mistakes, I commit to the following action steps to build my resiliency:

1. _____

2. _____

3. _____

DAY 4

FANTASTIC FAITH/ SPIRITUALITY

 ## Motivational Message

"Overcoming obstacles starts with an attitude that faith will see you through." - anonymous

 ## My Musings

A strong faith and sense of spirituality is regularly identified as a means of gaining peace, comfort and the strength to face trials in life.

Faith can also help one stay in touch with the sentiment that things happen for a reason. Prayer, meditation, and other spiritual disciplines can, amongst other things, serve to increase distress tolerance and provide hope.

As you examine adversity from your past, consider the role that faith/spirituality played in your personal journey. Reflect specifically if there were times that you faced obstacles in life when God or spiritual practices played an internal role in pulling you through. How specifically did they help?

_____

_____

_____

_____

_____

 Mindset Matters

Reflect on how getting in touch with the role that faith played in overcoming past obstacles could influence your mindset as you prepare for adversity you will inevitably face in the future?

_____

_____

_____

_____

_____

✓ Make it Happen

I will commit to the following action steps to strengthen my faith to bolster my resiliency:

1. _____

2. _____

3. _____

DAY 5

STRONG SUPPORT SYSTEM

 Motivational Message

"You can't achieve anything entirely by yourself. A support system is a requirement for basic human existence." - Micheal Schur

 My Musings

People need people. It is true that some people need people more than others. But we all need people in our lives. Some days we just want someone to have fun with. Other times we need someone to tell us we *can* when we start to believe that we *can't*. And particularly when going through hard times. It is vital to know who our friends are.

Spend a few minutes evaluating your support system. Who is available? Who is resourceful? Who is loyal? Who is compassionate and nurturing? List some names that you will be sure to have in your phone that you can reach out to in a moments notice when the goin' gets tough.

_____

_____

_____

_____

_____

🧠 Mindset Matters

Do you have a hard time asking for help? Have a fear of being judged? Problem with trust? Reflect on shifts that might be needed in your mindset needed for developing and accessing a support strong system.

_____

_____

_____

_____

_____

✔ Make it Happen

I will commit to the following action steps to strengthen my support system:

1. _____

2. _____

3. _____

Motivational Message

"What screws us up most in life is the picture in our head of how life is supposed to be." - Jeremy Bings

 My Musings

In CBT we have a term called "should statements." It refers to when that voice inside our head that tells us that life should be different. We consider them irrational because they have nothing to do with reality. The reality is that everyone has trials. The more we insist in our minds that "things should go smoothly for me" or "life shouldn't have so many curves," the more distressed we will feel when things go awry.

Consider your expectations regarding past struggles. Write them out in the form of "should statements." Think particularly about your beliefs regarding "fairness."

_____

_____

_____

_____

_____

 Mindset Matters

Consider how these expectations influence your emotional reactions to life's curves. Reflect on what changes to your mindset that might help you anticipate rocky roads ahead and be more conducive to bouncing back more quickly when your road unexpectedly bends in the future.

_____

_____

_____

_____

_____

 Make it Happen

I commit to the following action steps to build my resistance for when I encounter the curves of life in my future journey:

1. _____

2. _____

3. _____

A SENSE OF HUMOR

 Motivational Message

"Nobody can make you feel inferior without your consent."
- Eleanor Roosevelt

My Musings

Nobody can offend us without our consent either. To say we are only offended when we choose to be is perhaps a bit strong, but emphasizes the role that our thinking plays in our feelings and our responses. When building resilience, it is vital to have the skill of laughing at ourselves and others (in a non-mean-spirited way). The better we can get at not taking mistakes or criticisms too seriously, the quicker we will be able to light-heartedly move forward and try again.

Recall a time in your life when you took something too seriously. Reflect on how it affected your feelings of hurt, anger, and willingness to try something new?

_____

_____

_____

_____

_____

🔘 Mindset Matters

Pick a comment made to you in recent memory that was upsetting or a mistake that you made and examine how you could have shifted your mindset to take it less personally or even gotten a bit of a laugh over it. Then reflect on how you could adapt that attitude moving forward.

_____

_____

_____

_____

_____

✅ Make it Happen

In the spirit of cultivating my sense of humor, I commit to the following action steps to build my resilience:

1. _____

2. _____

3. _____

DAY 8

DRAW ON YOUR STRENGTHS

 ## Motivational Message

"Success is achieved by developing our strengths, not eliminating our weaknesses." - Marilyn vos Savant

🗨 My Musings

In doing therapy and coaching with clients for almost 25 years I have always had an expression those who worked with me became familiar with - "Arrows up, Arrows down." As one of my clients once put it, "Oh, you want me to work on not only having less bad, but also more good." Strengths harness the "good" that we all inherently have in us. These qualities can be powerful assets as we work towards becoming more resilient.

Strengths might include talents, personality traits, "gifts," or other internal attributes. Reflect on some of the specific strengths you have within you.

_____

_____

_____

_____

_____

Mindset Matters

Possessing gifts, strengths, and talents is of limited value if we aren't able to access these and use them to help us tackle life more effectively in some way. Intentionally consider how you might harness each in a specific way to help you overcome an obstacle you are currently facing or one that you anticipate on the horizon.

_____

_____

_____

_____

_____

Make it Happen

Specific action steps I will take to harness my strengths and help cultivate resilience in my life are:

1. _____

2. _____

3. _____

DAY 9

GIVE UP THE NEED TO SEE IMMEDIATE RESULTS

 ## Motivational Message

"The ability to discipline yourself to delay gratification in the short term in order to enjoy greater rewards in the long term is the indispensable pre-requisite for success." - Maxwell Maltz

My Musings

One of the most crucial tenets of motivation has to do with relinquishing the need for immediate gratification. Millions of people can relate with starting a new diet feeling invigorated on day one and defeated a week later, having already given up the habits necessary to achieve their goals. It is much better to walk one mile a day for ten days than to walk ten miles the first day and get on the scale the next morning expecting miraculous and immediate results. Reflect on an achievement in which sustained effort over time was worth it for you.

_____

_____

_____

_____

_____

Mindset Matters

Develop a marathon mindset. Nobody wins in the first mile. Cede the need to reap immediate rewards. On days it seems like it isn't worth it, remind yourself that if you continue to do the next right thing in the short term all your steps will be worth it in the long term. Consider how you might shift your mindset to cultivate this mentality.

_____

_____

_____

_____

_____

Make it Happen

I commit to take the following action steps to tackle a current problem I am facing to build my resilience, even though it doesn't "feel" like they are worth it in the short term:

1. _____

2. _____

3. _____

DAY 10
SEE CHALLENGES AS OPPORTUNITIES

 ## *Motivational Message*

"The pessimist sees difficulty in every opportunity. The optimist sees opportunity in every difficulty." - Winston Churchill

My Musings

Resilient people don't shy away from being challenged. In fact, many purposefully challenge themselves daily in some way. If we could view every struggle in life as a potential learning opportunity, we wouldn't dread them as much, and wouldn't submit ourselves to the unmerciful self-talk many endure when life gets hard. One of my clients who had a habit of saying "but Jeff it's hard" almost killed me (in an endearing way:)) when that phrase was regularly met with my excited voice countering with "Oh, I'm so excited for you - another opportunity for growth!"

_____

_____

_____

_____

_____

 Mindset Matters

Rather than taking drastic steps to avoid adversity, I coach clients to "want it," regularly asking the question "what can I learn from this challenge today?"

Consider ways could you change your mindset approach to facing challenges to build resilience.

_____

_____

_____

_____

_____

✓ Make it Happen

As a result of shifting my perspective on life's challenges, I commit to take the following action steps today to build upon my resilience:

1. _____

2. _____

3. _____

PIVOT

 Motivational Message

"A bend in the road is not the end of the road unless we fail to make the turn." - Helen Keller

My Musings

The word "pivot" has become all the rage in personal development and even career assessment and planning circles during this Covid season. A player must pivot in basketball when someone from the opposing team closely guards him and presents an obstacle to his passing or shooting lane. Such a move creates lanes of opportunity that were not available to him before the maneuver. Similarly, in life sometimes we need to be able to demonstrate the flexibility to adapt to unforeseen obstacles to create new "lanes of opportunity" for ourselves. This principle is important enough a version of it is #1 on the Connor-Davis Resilience Scale.

The possibility of pivoting resonates with me in the following way(s):

_____

_____

_____

_____

_____

🔊 *Mindset Matters*

Dr. Michael McGriffy is famous for saying "Blessed are the flexible, for they shall not be bent out of shape." Flexibility in thinking and behavior has been identified as one of the key factors in what makes a personality healthy.

Reflect on ways you could increase your flexibility in the face of unexpected circumstances.

_____

_____

_____

_____

_____

✓ *Make it Happen*

In an attempt to develop flexibility, I commit to the following action steps to build resilience:

1. _____

2. _____

3. _____

Motivational Message

"A setback is a setup for a comeback." - Willie Jollie

My Musings

This phrase made famous by best-selling author John C. Maxwell offers key wisdom in our quest to build resilience. Everyone fails in life. However it is how we think about those failures that determines if we fall back or fight back.

Reflect on one or more past failure(s) and lessons learned from them.

_____

_____

_____

_____

_____

Mindset Matters

Rick Warren famously penned "we are all products of our past, but we don't have to be prisoners to our past." Staying stuck in the past is incompatible with developing resilience. Consider a simple "fail" you had recently, and reflect on unproductive versus productive mindsets for responding to it.

_____

_____

_____

_____

_____

✓ Make it Happen

Taking into consideration my lessons learned, I commit to the following action steps to ensure that I fail forward and build resilience:

1. _____

2. _____

3. _____

DAY 13

AVOID THE VICTIM TRAP

 Motivational Message

"I am not what happened to me. I am what I choose to become."
- C.G. Jung

My Musings

There is a difference between being victimized and adopting a victim mentality. All human beings are victimized; some in small ways and some in heinous ways. Individual events involving legitimate victimization should be met with compassion, validation, and support. But people who continue to view themselves as powerless and take on entitlement or helpless victim-based identities set themselves up to lack resilience in life.

Reflect on ways in which you have been victimized in your life (in large or small ways).

_____

_____

_____

_____

_____

# Mindset Matters

As you reflect on the these events, consider whether you fell into the victim trap? Or did you come closer to developing a mindset that says "I can do something about future life challenges?" In what ways might your thinking need to change to move from a victim mindset to a victory mindset?

_____

_____

_____

_____

_____

Make it Happen

If my response to previous victimizations in life contributed to some learned helplessness, I commit to take the following action steps to empower myself and reverse my victim or entitled thinking:

1. _____

2. _____

3. _____

DAY 14

COMMIT TO A NEW HARD ACTION NO MATTER HOW UNCOMFORTABLE IT FEELS

 Motivational Message

"We change our behavior when the pain of staying the same outweighs the fear of change." - Tony Robbins

My Musings

Many of us humans stink at change. A client once told me "The abuse I do know is better than a life without it I don't know." We put up with a lot in life to maintain "familiar." Building resilience requires stepping out of our ruts we find ourselves in and committing to be something different.

Reflect on a situation in which you refuse(d) to leave your comfort zone and consequences you were willing to suffer because of it.

_____

_____

_____

_____

_____

 Mindset Matters

To overcome the "stuck" mindset, try doing a pros and cons exercise. Brainstorm and write down the advantages and disadvantages of continuing a current known suffering versus your anticipated predicted suffering. Reflect on your awarenesses.

_____

_____

_____

_____

_____

✔ Make it Happen

After considering the pros and cons, I commit to the following new action steps to develop resilience no matter how hard they are:

1. _____

2. _____

3. _____

KEEP YOUR EYES ON THE PRIZE

 Motivational Message

"When you focus on what you want, everything else falls way."
- Louise Armstrong

My Musings

It can be easy to lose heart. Many of us are easily distracted. Some become devastated by failure. Developing resilience involves staying the course no matter what. The best quarterbacks in football are said to have a "short memory" because after throwing an interception they can go right back on the field and give it another shot without losing confidence. Winning the game is all that matters.

Write down some goals you currently have that, when you are tempted to get derailed, you can remind yourself of to maintain motivation.

_____

_____

_____

_____

_____

🧠 Mindset Matters

What mantras or sayings can you incorporate into your thinking to help you stay the course when you are tempted to get off track? If you are a task-oriented person, recalling your goals to keep them 'top of mind' can help. Record them below, and also write them on a 3x5 card that can be put somewhere you will see it regularly to help gradually fortify your attitude of resilience.

_____

_____

_____

_____

_____

✔ Make it Happen

As I remind myself of my goals, I commit to take the following steps to stay the course and build resilience:

1. _____

2. _____

3. _____

Motivational Message

"When you feel like quitting, remember why you started."
- John di lemme

My Musings

Yesterday's entry ask you to consider goals as a way of maintaining motivation and cultivating resiliency. Many are motivated by goals, but others are motivated more by meaning. Reflect on what the most important things are in life to you. These might include values, relationships, or existential concerns.

Make a list of as many things that are meaningful to you as you can think of.

_____

_____

_____

_____

_____

 Mindset Matters

Viktor Frankl, who spent many years of his life in a concentration camp, believed that what was most important was "the meaning of a person's life in a given moment." Consider in what ways you might incorporate meaning into your every day mindset to foster resilience.

_____

_____

_____

_____

_____

 Make it Happen

I commit to take the following action steps to live my life consistent with my values, meaning, and sense of purpose:

1. _____

2. _____

3. _____

DIG DEEP

 ## Motivational Message

"Don't quit when you are tired, quit when you are done." - unknown

🗨 My Musings

Sometimes it feels like we have pushed ourselves until we can't push any more. But how do we really know? We only learn our real limits by reaching what we think they are - and then trying to exceed them! It is only when we attempt to go farther than we thought we could that self-limiting beliefs begin to change and we develop an increased sense of mastery and confidence.

Brainstorm some ways that you might push yourself through pain in the upcoming weeks.

_____

_____

_____

_____

_____

⊙ Mindset Matters

As you learn that you are capable of more than you thought you were, what are some ways that you can you incorporate this new knowledge about yourself into your resilience mindset?

_____

_____

_____

_____

_____

✓ Make it Happen

I commit to take the following action steps to "dig deep" this week. And when it feels like I might not be able to go any further, I will

1. _____

2. _____

3. _____

Motivational Message

"Going through things you never thought you'd go through will only take you to places you never thought you'd get to." - Morgan Harper Nichols

My Musings

I once worked with a man who had been shot by law enforcement while attempting to steal a police car during a drug bust gone bad. After 6 weeks in a coma, becoming100% blind, and completely losing his sense of smell, he has now been in recovery for 16 years. He shared this in a gratitude group at our psychiatric hospital. He now shares it regularly as part of a prison ministry.

What opportunities might you now be "uniquely qualified" for that you were not before having gone through your specific trial(s)?

_____

_____

_____

_____

_____

❤️ Mindset Matters

The man mentioned is now famous (around the hospital) for his statement "I believe God knew I had to be unconscious for six weeks to get off the stuff - I could have never kicked it on my own - I am so thankful. I see more now that I don't have any eyes than I ever did when I actually had them."

In what ways can you change your mindset in response to some of the things you have endured in life to reflect noticing a silver lining?

_____

_____

_____

_____

_____

✔️ Make it Happen

I commit to take the following action steps to help others, serve my community, or contribute to society sharing in some way the "gift" of my experience:

1. _____

2. _____

3. _____

Motivational Message

"Positive people are able to maintain a broader perspective and see the big picture which helps them identify solutions where as negative people maintain a negative perspective and focus on problems."
- Barbara Fredrickson

My Musings

We have all heard the expression "she couldn't see the forest for the trees," describing a person who is so focused on the details in front of their face that they miss the larger point. A big picture perspective is crucial when going through a pandemic, or any type of an extended time of difficulty.

I have heard Bob Leahy, the Director of the American Institute of Cognitive Therapy, encourage looking at the Covid-19 pandemic like a chapter in a book. We could view any extended trial in this way. As much as we might not like this chapter, remember it is very likely only a time-limited section in the novel that is our entire life. This too shall pass. Reflect on how you would like the NEXT chapters of your life to read.

_____

_____

_____

_____

_____

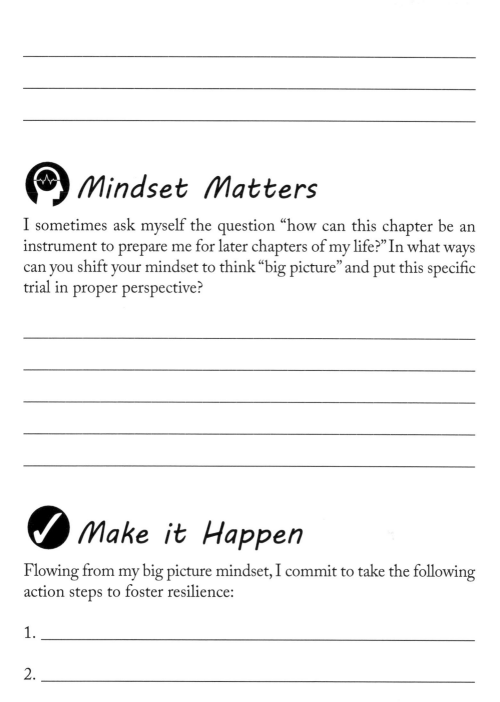 *Mindset Matters*

I sometimes ask myself the question "how can this chapter be an instrument to prepare me for later chapters of my life?" In what ways can you shift your mindset to think "big picture" and put this specific trial in proper perspective?

_____

_____

_____

_____

_____

✓ *Make it Happen*

Flowing from my big picture mindset, I commit to take the following action steps to foster resilience:

1. _____

2. _____

3. _____

COUNT YOUR BLESSINGS

 Motivational Message

"Thanks is the highest form of thought; and gratitude is happiness doubled by wonder." - CK Chesterton

My Musings

Research has suggested that gratitude can play important roles in helping a number of areas, from physical conditions to preventing relapse in depression. Being thankful is not always easy. But it is always best for us. Reflect on some of the things you have to be thankful for and record them below.

_____

_____

_____

_____

_____

 Mindset Matters

Some people I work with seem to think that being thankful for things they *do have* minimizes the pain they are experiencing resulting from

things they *don't have*. It is possible to be concerned about difficulties and thankful for blessings at the same time. Furthermore, even if ninety-nine things out of one hundred were going poorly in our lives, it would still be in our best interest emotionally to focus on the one that is going well. I started a game with my twins when they were 6 called the "bright side game" in which every time something bad happens the question is asked "what is the bright side?" of that particular event.

_____

_____

_____

_____

_____

Make it Happen

Identify one or more "bad" things that have happened recently or are currently happening in your life. Ask the question, "in what way(s) could this be "good?" for each. This can be challenging, but is powerful work towards cultivating a mindset of resilience.

1. _____

2. _____

3. _____

Motivational Message

"Hope is being able to see that there is light in spite of all of the darkness."
- Desmond Tutu

My Musings

A fundamental tenet of resilience is tied to hope. Once all hope is lost, resilience has no chance. Never, ever, ever give up. When you can't see any, find someone that can and borrow hope from them.

Reflect on a time in which you lost hope and why you never want to return to that place in the future.

_____

_____

_____

_____

_____

Mindset Matters

When one is hopeless, it is difficult to find even the smallest ray of hope. It can be helpful to make a list of things that give you hope during times when you *do* see them, so that at times when you *don't* you have a resource at your disposal to serve as a reminder.

Brainstorm as many things as you can that give you hope. These can apply to a particular situation, or to life in general. Record them in the space below and rewrite them on a 3x5 card so you can take them with you and have them at times you need their reminders most.

_____

_____

_____

_____

_____

Make it Happen

I commit to the following specific action steps to keep hope alive as I work to develop my resilience:

1. _____

2. _____

3. _____

Jeff Riggenbach, PhD is a 3 time best-selling author and speaker/trainer/coach with the John Maxwell Team who has presented at conferences in all 50 United States, the UK, Canada, Mexico, Australia, New Zealand, and South Africa.

He trained at the prestigious Beck Institute of Cognitive Therapy and Research and has devoted his entire career to developing advanced expertise in thinking and personality styles. After 20 years in the clinical world of psychology treating psychiatric patients with and training clinicians in cognitive behavioral therapy his recent work has centered around cultivating mindsets for effective communication in workplace, educational, and faith-based environments.

In addition to his professional background, Jeff has had two kidney transplants, so he knows well from personal experience what it takes to overcome obstacles in life.

Dr. Riggenbach is also a certified behavioral consultant with *Personality Insights* and his talks on *"Dealing with Difficult People"* routinely receive the highest evaluations by conference participants. Look for his book *"Disarming High-Conflict Personalities"* set to be be released in early 2021.

Contact Jeff and his team at events@jeffriggenbach.com to start the conversation about coaching or booking him to speak to your organization, school, or church.

Made in the USA
Middletown, DE
17 February 2023

25089173R00029